RUNNING AFTER SI

میرا پر چھائیوں کے پیچھے بھاگنا

by

Hifsa Ashraf

حفصہ اشرف

HUMAN
/KIND
PRESS

WILMINGTON, DE

Running After Shadows - In English And Urdu

Copyright © 2020 Hifsa Ashraf
Copyright © 2020 Human/Kind Press
Edited by Robin Smith and Shloka Shankar

ISBN 978-1-951675-05-9

First Edition December 2020
Printed in the United States

HUMAN/KIND PRESS
Wilmington, Delaware

www.humankindjournal.org

Cover art by Grix

Running After Shadows

A Collection of Haiku
Destigmatizing Mental Illness in Women

flying shadow
across the dark sea
my ultimate persona

اڑتا ہوا سایہ

سیاہ سمندر کے پار

میری حتمی شخصیت

anxieties . . .
seeing through
the river fog

اضطراب ...
جیسے دریا کی دُھند
سے پار دیکھنا

deep inside
the rain whirlpool
my inner voice

بارش کے بھنور
کی گہرائی میں
میری اندرونی آواز

self-denial . . .
seeking the light
without shadows

اِنکارِ ذات...
روشنی کی تلاش
سائے کے بغیر

prognosis—
she paints her feelings
in black and white

تشخیص —

وہ اپنے جذبات کو رنگ دیتی ہے

سیاہ اور سفید

blackout—
the intensity of
my threshold level

ہوش کا گُم ہونا—
میرے محسوس کرنے کی حد
کی شدت

ashes
in the cold wind . . .
carrion crows

راکھ

سرد ہوا میں ...

مُردار خور کوے

claustrophobia
squeezing inside
the inner darkness

بند جگہوں کا خوف
میں سکڑتے ہوئے
اندرونی تاریکی میں

a starling murmuration blends into the dark amnesia

بھولنے کی بیماری جیسے مینا کے جھنڈ کا اندھیرے سے ملاپ

entangled hair
curling around her face
lunar eclipse

اُلجھے ہوئے گیسو

اُسکے چہرے کے گرد لپٹے ہوئے

چاند گرہن

wood smoke . . .
the visibility
of anonymity

لکڑی کا دُھواں...

مرئیت
گُمنامی کی

layer
after layer
after layer
of black fog

delirium

پرت

در پرت

در پرت

سیاہ دھند

ذہنی خلفشار

traumatic memories—
her rocking chair squeaks
in the cold night

تکلیف دہ یادیں—
اُس کی جھُولا کُرسی کی چر چراہٹ
سرد رات میں

first step
on the misty bridge
owl's hoot

پہلا قدم
کُہر زدہ پُل پر
اُلو کی آواز

at the core
of her palm lines . . .
black hole

اُسکی ہاتھ کی لکیروں
کے مرکز میں ۔ ۔ ۔
بلیک ہول

migraine—
the far side
of a full moon

درِد شقیقہ ——

پورے چاند کا

تاریک پہلو

summer solstice . . .
spending more time
with my shadow

گر میوں میں اِنقلاب شمسی . . .

اور زیادہ وقت بیتانا

اپنے سائے کے ساتھ

insanity
above the mountain clouds
my inner screams

پاگل پن
پہاڑوں کے بادلوں سے بھی اُوپر
میری اندرونی چیخیں

withered rose
the dark scars
of her sacrifices

مُرجھایا ہوا گلاب
سیاہ زخموں کے نشانات
اُس کی قربانیوں کے

self-loathing
avoiding (eve)n
the foggy mirror

خود سے نفرت
یہاں تک کہ گریز کرنا
دُھندلے عکس سے

bipolar—
the silhouette of driftwood
on a windswept beach

دو قطبی مالیخولیا۔۔۔

باد آورد لکڑی کا ایک رُخی خاکہ

بادِ زدہ ساحل پر

evening shadows . . .
the things we deny
become more visible

شام کے سائے...
جن چیزوں کی ہم نفی کرتے ہیں
وہ اور نمایاں ہو جاتی ہیں

the last train deepening my heartbeat

آخری ٹرین میرے دل کی دھڑکن کو گہرا کرتے ہوئے

PTSD
shadows lengthen
over the sky's edge

پی ٹی ایس ڈی
سائیوں کا بڑھنا
آسمان کے کنارے تک

standing still
on the dark path . . .
my childhood fears

توقف

تاریک راستے پر...

میرے بچپن کے خوف

fading memories
of the family tree . . .
hospice window

شَجرہ نَسَب کی
مدھم پڑتی یادیں...
مریض خانہ کی کھڑکی

binge eating
long strands of spaghetti
lost in my thoughts

کھانے کی نا قابلِ برداشت خواہش

سپیگیتی کے لمبے لچھے

خیالات کی گہرائی میں

dappled sunlight
my unspoken words
on the wall

چتکبری دُھوپ
میرے ناگُفتہ الفاظ

دیوار پر

sleepless night—
window cracks slice
a full moon

بے خوابی—
کھڑکی میں دراڑیں
مہتاب کی قاشیں کرتے ہوئے

Schizophrenia—
chasing butterfly trails
into the woods

شیزوفرینیا—
تتلی کے راستے کی کھوج
جنگل میں

monochrome rain
seeping into the soil
acute stress

یک رنگی بارش

مٹی میں سراہیت کرتی ہوئی

شدید ذہنی دباؤ

brain fog
running after
s h h h a d o w s

دماغ کی دُھند
میں پرچھائیوں کے پیچھے
بھاگتے ہوئے

ACKNOWLEDGEMENTS

Thank you to the editors of the following venues where some of these pieces previously appeared: *Bleached Butterfly, Cattails, Failed Haiku,* The Haiku Foundation's *Haiku Dialogue, haikuniverse,* and *The Zen Space.*

A special thanks to Robin Anna Smith, the editor of Human/Kind Journal for her encouragement and immense support. She made it possible for me to share my voice to the masses through this chapbook.

I also want to thank all those fellow poets who always encouraged me to write by giving their constructive feedback on my work.

I wish to thank those who have published my work, and all editors, journals, presses that support writers around the world.

ABOUT THE AUTHOR

Hifsa Ashraf lives in Rawalpindi, Pakistan. She was one of the finalists for the Sable Books Haiku Book Contest for Women (2020), and is an award-winning poet, and story writer. She is an editor and a founder of a bilingual online magazine *Saawan Rut* that promotes the short forms of creative writing. She is also an editor at *Haiku Commentary* blog. She writes poetry in English, Urdu, and Punjabi. Her first individual chapbook about workplace Islamophobia is *Working with Demons* (Proletaria Publishing, 2020). Her first collaborative chapbook with Alan Summers is *The Comfort of Crows* (Velvet Dusk Publishing, 2019).

Please visit her website (www.saawanrut.org) or blog (hifsays.blogspot.com) to view her published work. Or follow her on Twitter at @hifsays.

CPSIA information can be obtained
at www.ICGtesting.com
Printed in the USA
LVHW021647050121
675554LV00013B/726

9 781951 675059